LITTLE QUICK FIX:

GET YOUR DATA FROM EXPERIMENTS

#LittleQuickFix

Sara Miller McCune founded SAGE Publishing in 1965 to support the dissemination of usable knowledge and educate a global community. SAGE publishes more than 1000 journals and over 800 new books each year, spanning a wide range of subject areas. Our growing selection of library products includes archives, data, case studies and video. SAGE remains majority owned by our founder and after her lifetime will become owned by a charitable trust that secures the company's continued independence.

Los Angeles | London | New Delhi | Singapore | Washington DC | Melbourne

LITTLE QUICK FIX:

GET YOUR DATA FROM EXPERIMENTS

Helen
Coleman

Los Angeles | London | New Delhi
Singapore | Washington DC | Melbourne

Los Angeles | London | New Delhi
Singapore | Washington DC | Melbourne

SAGE Publications Ltd
1 Oliver's Yard
55 City Road
London EC1Y 1SP

SAGE Publications Inc.
2455 Teller Road
Thousand Oaks, California 91320

SAGE Publications India Pvt Ltd
B 1/I 1 Mohan Cooperative Industrial Area
Mathura Road
New Delhi 110 044

SAGE Publications Asia-Pacific Pte Ltd
3 Church Street
#10-04 Samsung Hub
Singapore 049483

Editor: Alysha Owen
Assistant editor: Lauren Jacobs
Senior project editor: Chris Marke
Marketing manager: Ben Sherwood
Cover design: Shaun Mercier
Typeset by: C&M Digitals (P) Ltd, Chennai, India
Printed in the UK

Library of Congress Control Number: 2020942785

British Library Cataloguing in Publication data

A catalogue record for this book is available from
the British Library

ISBN 978-1-5297-3592-5 (pbk)

At SAGE we take sustainability seriously. Most of our products are printed in the UK using responsibly
sourced papers and boards. When we print overseas we ensure sustainable papers are used as measured
by the PREPS grading system. We undertake an annual audit to monitor our sustainability.

Contents

2 MIN summary

Everything in this book!

Section 1 An experiment is testing your hypothesis or theory, **to discover if what you think is happening, is happening or not.**

Section 2 You need a well-designed experiment to provide the evidence **to support your interpretation of your hypothesis or theory.**

Section 3 There are 3 types of experiment to choose from. **There are Laboratory/Controlled Experiments, Field Experiments and Natural Experiments.**

Section 4 **To be ethical, you need to** know your subject, be honest and adhere to the correct, subject-specific codes of conduct.

Section 5 Your experiment needs to be reproducible. This means you need to be precise, detailed, honest and open about your processes, methods, observations, and any other important elements.

Section 6 Knowing your subject means you can plan the best version of your experiment and minimise systematic errors and reduce random errors.

Section 7 In experiments, you need to collect as much data as possible about the variables relevant to your hypothesis or theory.

Section 8 It's essential to collect and record data honestly, and correctly, in line with the chosen method, so your work can contribute as a valid addition to the body of knowledge in the subject.

Section

1

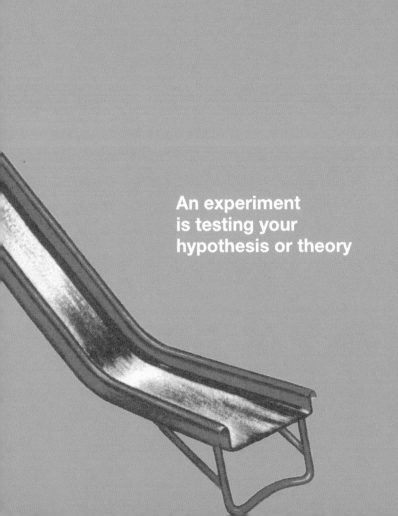

An experiment
is testing your
hypothesis or theory

What is an experiment?

An experiment is an accepted method of collecting data to test your hypothesis or theory. Experiments are rigorous, systematic and follow accepted processes.

An experiment is a way of carrying out research under controlled conditions

By isolating a specific independent variable, you can manipulate it to observe and measure the effect on the dependent variable, thereby testing your hypothesis or theory.

In practice there may be other variables you should be aware of and either control or investigate at the same time. Prior knowledge of the subject area will guide you as to what you should be looking for.

It is vital to conduct an experiment with as little bias and prejudice as possible, whilst showing you have thoroughly examined your hypothesis or theory and drawn correct assumptions from the data you have collected. The only way to do this is to follow the established methods in your discipline correctly and systematically.

AN EXPERIMENT TESTS A HYPOTHESIS OR THEORY

An experiment is the most efficient, scientifically accepted, method of testing your hypothesis or theory. A hypothesis, sometimes called the alternate or experimental hypothesis, is usually a statement, often tentatively made, about a possible relationship between two or more variables. Your hypothesis would commonly predict what you expect the outcome of your experiment to show. This hypothesis is often balanced by a null hypothesis, which predicts there is no relationship between the variables you have specified. Your hypothesis should be testable, precise and, typically, based on a specific property or relationship of the variables you are investigating.

A hypothesis is usually derived from a research question, but it is never a question itself, it is always a testable statement.

- Research question – Do students who revise achieve better grades?

- Hypothesis – Students who revise achieve better grades.

- Null hypothesis – Students who revise do not achieve better grades.

MAINTAINING CONTROL

In an ideal world you would be able to conduct all experiments in a laboratory or under completely controlled conditions. This would enable you to have absolute certainty over any possible cause and effect relationship. In the real world, it is not often feasible to study your subject in these conditions, so you have to attempt to maintain as much control as manageable whilst recognising as many of the limitations or possible variables as you can.

WHAT IS A VARIABLE?

A variable is anything and everything that can vary in an experiment, some of which you will be able to manipulate or modify. There are different types of variables.

- Independent variable – this is the one, or more, things you are manipulating during your experiment.

- Dependent variable – the one you observe to measure the effect of the independent variable.

- Controlled/Constant variables – the things you are controlling or keeping constant in order to ensure they do not affect your experiment.

- Extraneous variables – something that happens which you didn't plan for and so failed to plan for it to be controlled.

- Confounding variables – something that alters or influences both the independent and dependent variable to confound the actual relationship, or give a spurious relationship.

EXPERIMENTS NEED TO BE OBJECTIVE

Experiments need to be objective, which means you need to minimise bias and reduce prejudice as much as you can. The best way of doing this is to approach your experiment systematically and with as much prior knowledge as possible. Engaging with a standardised process, such as the scientific method if it is appropriate for your area, should help you to focus on the facts and filter out any conscious or unconscious bias and prejudice you may have.

When you are planning your next experiment, check to find out what the usual systems are for your subject area and ensure you stick to them.

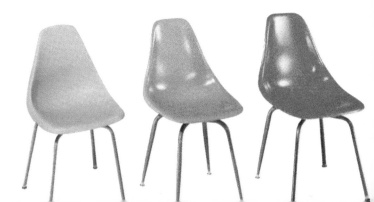

For your next experiment, please have a go at identifying the variables in your experiment and completing the following checkpoint task.

In this example, the experiment is based on the final weight of strawberries and its relationship to the amount of fertiliser applied to the soil during the growing period of the strawberry plant.

Variable type	Example	Now it's your opportunity to have a go!
Independent variable:	Amount of fertiliser	
Dependent variable:	Weight of the strawberry	
Controlled/ Constant variables:	Sunlight, temperature, water, wind, bugs, disease, etc.	
Confounding variables:	Other soil properties/ variations, individual genetic differences between the plants, not hulling the strawberries equally, etc.	
Anything else that could influence your variables:	Incorrect weighing of the amount of fertiliser, incorrect weighing of the mass of the strawberry, etc.	

2 Section

You need a well-designed experiment

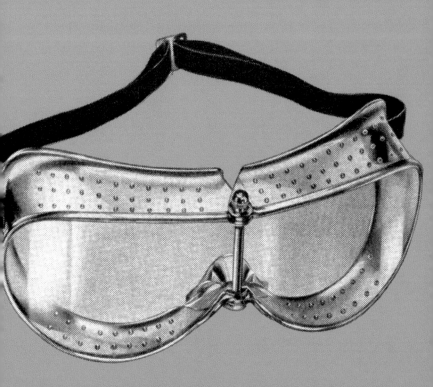

Why do I need to do an experiment for my research?

summary

A clearly defined, well-constructed
experiment is recognised as the only efficient
and scientific method of collecting evidence
supporting your interpretation of your
hypothesis or theory.

Correctly conducted experiments are the most efficient, scientifically recognised method of gathering evidence to support your hypothesis or theory

Experiments must adhere to specific protocols to ensure the results are accepted as being valid and not caused by some other extraneous variable. By conducting an experiment, you will have to ensure your experiment does too, and this supports your evidence in being accepted as a valid contribution to your area of research.

Carrying out an experiment correctly, not only shows your evidence is valid, but also shows you have engaged with the proper behaviours and conduct appropriate to your subject. This can only be achieved when you know your subject in depth and have thoroughly planned your experiment.

We have all these ideas about the natural world, how people interact, what is happening around us, what is happening inside us, how does one thing interact or affect another, and so on. However, to turn these theories into knowledge that we can trust we need valid and reliable evidence. To do this we conduct an experiment, but conducting an experiment can be a daunting task to undertake. Although, with the proper planning and adherence to appropriate protocols, the results will usually make it worth the effort.

THE PRIMARY ROLE OF AN EXPERIMENT IS TO TEST YOUR HYPOTHESIS OR THEORY

Irrelevant of the area of research you are engaging with, an experiment allows you to investigate whether your ideas about how something works or interacts with something else is a correct theory that matches what happens. This knowledge can then help to spur you, or others, on to develop further theories and knowledge. Experiments are a recognised part of science and, more specifically, part of what is called the scientific method.

YOUR
EXPERIMENT
WILL HELP YOU
UNDERSTAND
IF YOU ARE
CORRECT
IN YOUR
ASSUMPTIONS

The scientific method is the process of gathering empirical data in an effort to test a hypothesis or theory. It's generally accepted there are five stages in the scientific method. However, it is possible to find this presented in more or fewer stages, depending on where you find your information, although it is still the same process.

THE SCIENTIFIC METHOD

The stages are broadly broken down into:

1 making an observation or finding a topic of interest

2 formulating hypotheses

3 making deductions from the hypotheses

4 testing the deductions via an experiment

5 modifying the hypotheses if necessary.

Sometimes you may need to repeat this cycle until you arrive at a satisfactory end-point.

Including an appropriate and properly performed experiment in your research is the best way to gather evidence supporting your hypothesis or theory, but it is also the best way to show you are a credible researcher in your chosen field. Just make sure you conduct it correctly, that it is appropriate to your area of research and you adhere to the proper codes of conduct.

Looking back at the previous section, we can construct a hypothesis and a null hypothesis related to the variables from the experiment you envisaged and listed.

The easiest way to start formulating your hypothesis is to complete the following sentence but with your own choice of variables and consider what relationship are you identifying.

If ... [I do this/ independent variable]

..., then

... [this/ dependent variable]

... will happen.

Write in your hypothesis below:

If ..., then

... will happen.

2 When you consider this sentence, including your variables, it will help to highlight the relationship between the two variables. This helps you to create your hypothesis, and your null hypothesis, which is the statement showing there is no relationship between the two variables.

Examples of both of these variables are shown in the steps below.

Steps	Example	Your go!
Basic idea	If I add more fertiliser to the soil (independent variable) then the mass of strawberries at the end of the experiment will alter (dependent variable).	
Hypothesis	There is a relationship between the amount of fertiliser added to the soil and the final mass of strawberries produced.	
Null hypothesis	There is no relationship between the amount of fertiliser added to the soil and the final mass of strawberries produced.	

What is the correct sequence of the scientific method?

Put them in the correct order below.

formulating hypotheses

making an observation or finding a topic of interest

modifying the hypotheses if necessary.

making deductions from the hypotheses

testing the deductions via an experiment

1 ....

2 ....

3 ....

4 ....

5 ....

ANSWERS

CHECKPOINT

1. making an observation or finding a topic of interest ....
2. formulating hypotheses ....
3. making deductions from the hypotheses ....
4. testing the deductions via an experiment ....
5. modifying the hypotheses if necessary. ....

Section

Three types of experiment

What types of experiment are there?

summary

Experiments are usually
split into 3 main types:
Natural Experiments,
Field Experiments and
Laboratory/Controlled Experiments.

Different situations and subjects demand different types of experiment

It is not always possible to study your research sample in a laboratory or other research setting affording controlled conditions. This means you have to be aware of the different types of experiment in order to choose the most appropriate experiment for your research and your sample.

The following three types of experiment cover, pretty much, every possible type of investigation you can imagine, but with one of the main differences being the levels of control available to the researcher.

Natural experiments offer the lowest levels of control, with Field experiments affording limited control and Laboratory/Controlled experiments demanding the highest levels of control.

Natural, Field and Laboratory/Controlled experiments have many elements in common. The three types of experiment are all conventional methods of collecting data to test your hypothesis or theory and they are rigorous, systematic and follow accepted processes. However, the key difference is the level of control afforded to the researcher, and that is dictated by the subject and the sample. The three types of experiment are equally valid as long as they are used for the appropriate situation.

In a Natural experiment the research is conducted in the natural setting, but the researcher has no control over how the independent variable behaves or acts. This is appropriate for researching something in its own natural setting when you need to observe the true behaviour of the independent variable. The absence of control reduces the possibility of bias, while also using the natural setting of the independent variable, which means Natural experiments are recognised to have a high level of ecological validity.

THERE ARE CHALLENGES TO BE FACED WITH NATURAL EXPERIMENTS

Replicating the study can be challenging, if not impossible, as in addition to having no control over the independent variable, the researcher has no control over any extraneous variables and you are using a natural setting. It can take a long time to blend into the background enough to research something in its natural setting without having any impact, so a Natural experiment can be quite a time-consuming and expensive process.

FIELD EXPERIMENTS ARE THE MIDDLE GROUND

Field experiments are the middle ground between Natural experiments and Laboratory/Controlled experiments. Field experiments take place in the natural setting and the researcher does manipulate the independent variable. As with a Natural experiment, there is a possibility of less bias and a higher level of ecological validity, than in a Laboratory/Controlled experiment, because the independent variable is in its own natural setting. However, again it can be difficult to replicate due to using a natural setting and the lack of control over extraneous variables.

LABORATORY EXPERIMENTS ARE THE 'GOLD STANDARD'

Laboratory/Controlled experiments are still often perceived as the 'gold standard' of experiments and can produce the most accurate results, due to being performed under such highly controlled conditions. Although often referred to as Laboratory/Controlled experiments, it is important to note they don't have to take place in a laboratory, just under conditions that are very well controlled. The researcher precisely controls the independent variable, the conditions under which the experiment is conducted and the extraneous variables. This does mean the experiment can struggle from bias and low ecological validity.

The level of control in this type of experiment means it can be quite easy to replicate the experiment and it is often possible to establish a cause and effect relationship. However, the high level of control also requires a high level of planning and effort to create a truly controlled situation, which can be both time consuming and expensive.

Type of experiment	Highlights	Challenges
Natural	Able to investigate the true behaviour of the sample in its natural setting High ecological validity Low possibility of bias	Difficult to replicate No control over independent variable No control over extraneous variables Time consuming Expensive
Field	Able to investigate the sample in its natural setting Control over independent variable High ecological validity	Difficult to replicate No control over extraneous variables Some possibility of bias Time consuming Expensive
Laboratory / Controlled	Easy to replicate Control over independent variable Control over extraneous variables Able to establish a cause and effect relationship	Low ecological validity High possibility of bias Time consuming Expensive

It's important to know enough about each type of experiment to make an informed choice and choose the one that best fits your needs. However, if in doubt, the following flow chart should help you to really make your mind up!

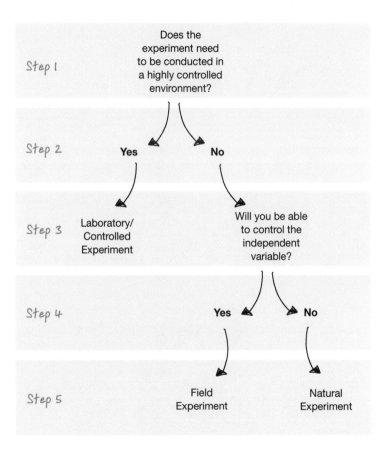

Step 1 — Does the experiment need to be conducted in a highly controlled environment?

Step 2 — **Yes** / **No**

Step 3 — Laboratory/Controlled Experiment

Will you be able to control the independent variable?

Step 4 — **Yes** / **No**

Step 5 — Field Experiment / Natural Experiment

45

THE TYPE OF EXPERIMENT
I WILL CONDUCT IS

....

CONGRATULATIONS

YOU HAVE NOW TAKEN
THE FIRST STEP TO DESIGNING
YOUR EXPERIMENT.

How to be ethical

1

Section

How do I ensure my experiment is ethically appropriate?

summary

It's possible to ensure an experiment is ethically appropriate simply by adhering to the correct rules of conduct for the area of research.

summary

Experiments must be ethical

Experiments must always adhere to the appropriate set of ethical rules of conduct created or governed by the area in which the research is taking place. By doing so you respect the welfare, rights and dignity of all concerned. This supports the credibility of your experiment, your research and you.

It's actually very easy to ensure experiments are conducted in an ethically correct manner. If you know your subject, understand your subject area and behave respectfully, honestly and responsibly, while following the correct codes of conduct for your subject area, you will probably be ethically appropriate.

It is a fundamental requirement of a legally acceptable experiment to ensure it is conducted in an ethically correct and appropriate manner. It's your duty to be considerate of the rights, welfare and dignity of all concerned, ensuring no harm is done to any participants. It's also necessary to guarantee all data is handled correctly according to the appropriate data protection regulations or guidelines. Additionally, the confidentiality of all participants must be respected, and you must behave honestly, with integrity and take responsibility for your actions. These are some of the basic ethical considerations and they're vital for your reputation, that of your institution, and for the legality of your work.

IT'S YOUR DUTY
TO BE ETHICAL

The first step towards being ethically appropriate, is finding the correct ethical code / codes of conduct for your subject area. If you're a student, then there will probably be a specific code of conduct created by your institution, or funding body. Your tutors or colleagues should be able to guide you on this. Some areas have very specific requirements, for example the National Health Service in England, Wales and Scotland (NHS), may require you to submit your proposal for review by an NHS Research Ethics Committee.

FIND YOUR
ETHICAL CODE

Irrelevant of your subject area, you will probably have to complete a detailed ethics form, specifying elements of your proposed experiment. This will likely include why you wish to conduct an experiment in your subject, how you intend to run it, any possible harm that might happen and the precautionary measures you intend to take. Risk assessments can feature heavily in your research proposals and experiments, so have a go at the one in the checkpoint at the end of this section.

COMPLETE AN ETHICS FORM

If you are collecting data from people, it's necessary to gain fully informed consent prior to data collection, if possible. Unless you're conducting covert research, for which you will still need full ethical approval, you must seek the approval of the participant to engage in your experiment. This involves explaining to that person, in detail, as much as possible about the experiment, what any procedures may involve, and all possible outcomes or experiences they may undergo. The participant should be informed of what is going to happen to their data from the experiment and feel comfortable knowing they can withdraw from the experiment at any time, without penalty.

GAIN INFORMED CONSENT

Protecting the identity and data of your participants is also a fundamental requirement of ethically correct experiments. It's essential to consider how you are going to protect the identity of your participants and maintain data from your experiment in a confidential manner, in line with the appropriate regulations. Your tutors and colleagues should be able to help you with this too, so pay attention to their guidance and please treat people with respect and protect them from harm. Revealing someone's identity can have devastating consequences for them, so please be careful.

It's important to remember animal studies are also included in requiring ethical approval and ethical guidelines will likely be guided by a specific body. For example, the UK adheres to the Animals Scientific Procedures Act (1986). This states it's illegal to use an animal for research where there is a possible alternative and the expected benefits must outweigh any possible adverse effects.

PROTECT
IDENTITIES

The only way to really know you're conducting an ethically appropriate experiment is if you know your subject and behave correctly. If you know your subject, then you can be competent enough to identify possible areas where harm may occur and assess how to avoid them. Conducting yourself and your experiment honestly, respectfully and responsibly, whilst adhering to the correct, subject-specific codes of conduct, will enable you to ensure your experiment is ethically appropriate.

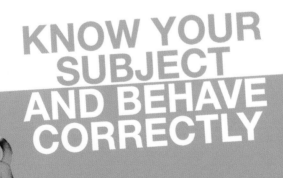

KNOW YOUR SUBJECT AND BEHAVE CORRECTLY

Even if your research does not need ethical approval, please remember you will still need to complete a Risk Assessment. A Risk Assessment is concerned with identifying any possible risks associated with your experiment or research, and the actions you could take to mitigate those risks. Completing a Risk Assessment will help to focus your mind on any health and safety issues and solutions for you and everyone included in your research. There may be a specific form to be completed at your institution or even risk assessment training, so ask around.

RISK ASSESSMENTS

ASSESS THE RISKS

When planning your next experiment, start practising on the following Risk Assessment, with at least five of your own examples to help you consider possible risks and mitigating actions. To help even further with

Example:

		1.	2.
Possible hazards	Slip, trips and falls		
Who may be harmed and how	Colleagues, participants, visitors, observers.		
Level of risk High/Medium/Low	Medium		
Action required	Ensure everyone attending the area will be advised to wear suitable footwear. All walkways to be kept clear of debris and possible trip hazards. Check all areas are well-lit.		
Who assigned to complete action	All		
Date action must be completed	With immediate effect onwards.		
Action completed Y/N	Y		

completing this, and all future Risk Assessments, please check with the local Health and Safety regulations in your area.

	4.	5.

Section

5

**Your experiment needs
to be reproducible**

How do I make my experiment reproducible?

Paying attention to the fine details, strictly adhering to your methodology, and being open and honest, will help to make your experiment reproducible.

Being reproducible is one of the fundamental requirements of every scientific study

When someone else is able to reproduce the experiment you have created and gain the same/similar results from the same/similar input, then this shows you've conducted your experiment with proper scientific rigour and your measures are considered reliable. It shows your results are consistent and not just the product of some other extraneous variable.

Ensuring your experiment is reproducible is an essential part of the process and is all about being open, honest and specific, and precisely sticking to the experimental design.

PLAN
APPROPRIATELY

Making sure your experiment is reproducible is a lot easier than most people think.

It just takes time in the planning stages, discipline during the process, and honesty about the results. When you plan your experiment you have to think and plan the whole process through very carefully, paying attention to even the smallest of details. Take time to consider what might be any possible choices at any given point and what you want to achieve. Spending time in the planning stage and removing all possibility of vagueness will save you time during your experiment and support your work being reproducible.

PERFECT YOUR RECIPE

Your plan is your precise recipe and this is the recipe someone else will use to conduct their version of your experiment. Remember that if someone else wishes to reproduce your experiment, which is what you want, then it's unlikely they'll be able to contact you and ask a question. Additionally, it is part of your role to ensure everyone else has the correct level of detail to reproduce your experiment. This means you need to be meticulous in detailing your procedures.

Once you've meticulously planned your experiment, you need to conscientiously and methodically adhere to that plan or note fully any changes as you make them. Be strict about adhering to your guidelines as this is important, but also recognise that real life does happen and if it's not possible to maintain your original procedure, because you've encountered something unplanned, then be honest and open about all the changes you've had to make.

PAY
ATTENTION

When collecting your results, really pay attention and make sure you genuinely see and record your actual results with clarity and honesty. It can be tempting to 'see what you want to see' when you have conducted an experiment or sometimes even record the data incorrectly. This is not through intent, but simply wishful thinking, so focus, be as objective as possible and do not attempt to 'read between the lines'. Just because you may not have achieved the results you wished, wanted or expected, doesn't mean your experiment was wrong!

REMEMBER REPRODUCIBILITY AND REPLICATION ARE NOT THE SAME!

Reproducibility is concerned with another researcher reproducing your experiment and achieving the same or substantially the same results. Replication, however, is a feature of your experimental design where you may wish to repeat certain parts of your experiment. To create a reproducible experiment, plan carefully and stick to it, record carefully and disclose any alterations, and record your data accurately.

Consider the following diagram for your next experiment to ensure it's reproducible.

1) Who will be involved?

8) Any other resources?

7) Any other points for consideration?

6) Length of time for experiment?

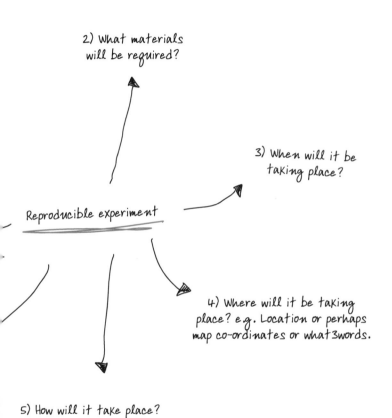

2) What materials
will be required?

3) When will it be
taking place?

Reproducible experiment

4) Where will it be taking
place? e.g. Location or perhaps
map co-ordinates or what3words.

5) How will it take place?

6

Plan the best version
of your experiment

How do I minimise error?

Minimising error in
your experiments is all
about careful design,
precision and analysis.

The danger of error appearing in your experiment is ever present, but it is possible to reduce its effect to a minimum

By knowing your subject, you will be able to pinpoint the areas where error can creep into your experiment and either prevent it, make allowances for it, or quantify it and its effect.

There are different types of error and it is not possible to completely eradicate all error from your experiment. However, if you are sufficiently vigilant throughout your design, experiment and analysis, you will be able to minimise it and reduce its deleterious influence.

TRY TO
MINIMISE ERROR

It is not possible to measure anything exactly. However, it's up to you to make sure your results are not as wrong as they could be! All experiments suffer from error to some degree and that's ok. Nonetheless, it is possible to minimise error and you must show you've taken every possible step to do just that. As with every other aspect of experiments, knowing your subject, paying attention to your design, being precise, analysing data honestly with objectivity and adhering to the proper guidelines are all key parts to reducing the damage error may cause to your results.

The first point to focus on is understanding the types of error, what they are and where they might appear in your experiment. Experimental error is generally split into two types, systematic errors and random errors.

- Systematic errors
- Random errors

SYSTEMATIC ERRORS

Systematic errors are caused by something happening at the very core of the experiment. This can be as simple as using the incorrect measurement tool for something or an incorrectly calibrated instrument. It could even be consistently sampling an incorrect group of people for the experiment you're conducting. Whatever it is, it is something that has gone wrong on a basic level within the design of the experimental procedure and is consistently affecting the measurements collected by the same amount every time.

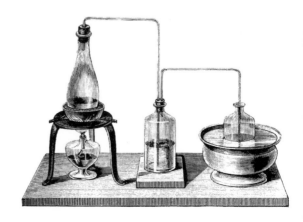

RANDOM
ERRORS

Random errors are caused by chance variations over which you may have little, if any, control. Random errors can be high or low, intermittent, present on one occasion and not the next, hard to fathom and hard to find. They can happen in the measuring instruments or in the environment. Basically they are called random for a reason, they happen at random! They can affect every measurement collected, but by a different amount every time.

REDUCING BOTH TYPES OF ERROR CAN BE SIMPLE

Reducing systematic errors is achieved by recognising the error and altering the design of the experimental procedure to eliminate it. Identifying a systematic error can be challenging because you conduct the experiment assuming the tools and system are free of errors. Isolating specific parts of the experiment or equipment and using a simplified technique with a standard, known result will help to pinpoint the location of the systematic error. The effect of random errors can be minimised by being precise with your experiment and measurements. Additionally, increasing the size of your sample and averaging the results will also average out any error and reduce the impact a random error can have.

IT IS EXPECTED THERE WILL BE SOME LEVEL OF ERROR IN YOUR EXPERIMENT

However, knowing your subject, careful planning, attention to detail, precision and honest data analysis, means you can plan the best version of your experiment and you will be able to minimise the possibility of any random and systematic errors.

To help you get to grips with the differences between systematic and random error, please allocate each of the following examples to the column you feel it belongs to.

1. Volt meter has not been zeroed correctly

2. Weighing scales consistently over weight

3. Taking a poll of voting behaviour outside a polling station when it is raining

4. Participants in a study happen to be friends on social media

5. 'Human error'

CHECKPOINT

Systematic Error	Random Error

Systematic Error	Random Error
Volt meter has not been zeroed correctly	Taking a poll of voting behaviour outside a polling station when it is raining
Weighing scales consistently over weight	Participants in a study happen to be friends on social media

Human error can be the cause of either random or systematic errors.

CONGRATULATIONS

YOU ARE NOW EQUIPPED TO CARRY OUT AN ETHICALLY SAFE AND SOUND EXPERIMENT WITH MINIMAL ERROR.

Section

7

Collect as much
data as possible

What types of data should I be collecting in an experiment?

summary

Generally speaking, you will be aiming to collect quantitative data or qualitative data, or a mix of both, depending on the experiment you are conducting.

Quantitative, Qualitative or both

To know what types of data you should be collecting in your experiment means you need to understand your subject, what types of data exist and which are appropriate for your experiment and analysis.

There are two main types of data and these are recognised as Quantitative data and Qualitative data. Both Quantitative and Qualitative data are then further subdivided. The type of data you should be collecting, whether quantitative or qualitative or both, depends on your field of research, your experiment, and the type of analysis you wish to conduct.

In your experiment you should aim to collect as much data as you feasibly can, whilst ensuring it's relevant to your hypothesis or theory. Deciding which data to collect is all about considering what type of information you need to address your hypothesis or theory. You'll also have to consider other factors such as time, finances, sample size, location and availability of support to conduct the research.

COLLECT LOTS OF RELEVANT DATA

If you are seeking to measure something numerically in an objective manner, then you'll probably engage with quantitative research. If you are looking to gather more descriptive data, which can be observed subjectively, then you'll likely be engaging with a qualitative approach. Perhaps you may even have the luxury of enough time to seek a fully rounded picture and use a mixed methods approach where you gather both quantitative and qualitative data. Either way, it really does depend on which approach fits in with your subject and experiment.

DIFFERENT SUBJECTS REQUIRE DIFFERENT TYPES OF DATA COLLECTION

Quantitative data is an umbrella heading for data primarily associated with numbers and subjects, which you can analyse objectively. This is the route if you're focusing on measurements or counts, for example heights, weights, temperatures, costs, areas, volumes, etc.

Quantitative data is further subdivided into continuous and discrete data. Continuous data is something that would take an infinite amount of time to count or something you can't count, whereas it's possible to count discrete data in a finite amount of time. An example of continuous data is age. You can't count age because it would take forever, for example 44 years, 3 months, 2 days, 5 hours, 8 seconds, … and so on. Examples of discrete data are money in your pocket or bank account or a person's age in years, etc.

QUANTITATIVE
DATA

Qualitative data is the umbrella heading for data primarily associated with characteristics, feelings and subjects, which should be considered subjectively. This is the route if you're focusing on perceptions, or viewpoints, for example sensations, feelings, opinions, etc. Qualitative data is further subdivided into nominal/ categorical data, binary data and ordinal data. Nominal/categorical data is when you name or categorise data without attributing it with a quantitative value, for example grouping together all the sweets from a bag of Starburst according to their colour (there is no value or rank to the colour) or coding interview transcripts into themes (the themes do not have a numeric value). A special case of categorical data is binary data. This is when there are two mutually exclusive categories and the data can only fit in one category, for example yes/no, on/off, agree/disagree, etc. Ordinal data is all about scales and is when data does have some sort of natural order or hierarchical structure to it, for example months of the year or response on a Likert scale, etc.

QUALITATIVE
DATA

Data is everything and it's everywhere; however, it's part of your role to fathom which data is appropriate for your experiment. This will be guided by the subject area you are studying, the type of experiment design you are engaging with and the analysis you wish to perform. Don't feel you have to stick to qualitative or quantitative, you can mix the data types if you need to.

DATA IS EVERYTHING AND IT'S EVERYWHERE

For each of the following categories have a think about what each one means and give three examples of each.

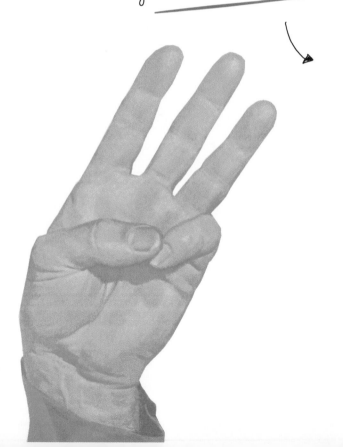

Discrete Data	Continuous Data
Example: Age in years	Example: Age
1	
2	
3	

Section

8

**Collect and record
data honestly**

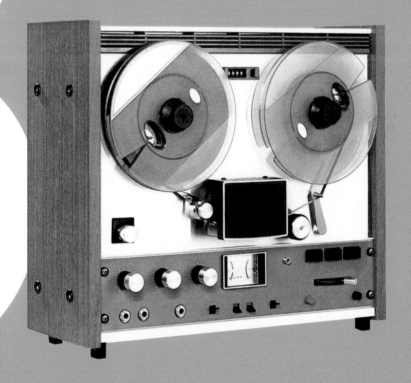

How do I collect and record data in an experiment?

summary

In an experiment you must collect and record data, systematically and methodically, from the sources you identify as appropriate for your experiment and analysis.

Collecting and recording data correctly for an experiment is vital if it's to be recognised as valid evidence for supporting your hypothesis or theory

How you collect and record the data will be guided by the type of data you are seeking to collect and record, the subject you are researching and the type of analysis you wish to perform.

There are many methods of data collection and the one you choose depends on your subject, availability of resources and how you will be conducting your research. Some of the main data collection methods are measurements, interviews, observations, published literature and questionnaires/surveys. The data collection method you choose will usually guide how you correctly record data for your experiment.

COLLECT AND RECORD DATA CORRECTLY

Ensuring you collect and record data correctly in an experiment is crucial to supporting your work in contributing to the body of knowledge in the subject. Collecting and recording data can be conducted via several different methods. However, irrelevant of how you go about it, you must conduct data collection honestly and as precisely as you can. Take care in everything you do, check any equipment you use, making sure it works and you're comfortable using it, and plan meticulously.

When you conduct any experiment you have to ensure you collect adequate data that is properly recorded. The data collection and recording methods you use depend on the experiment you are conducting, and the type of data you are seeking, as each data collection method will provide different types of data.

INTERVIEWS

Interviews are a method of qualitative data collection and can be performed in many different ways. Interviews can be structured, semi-structured or unstructured, they can be on a one-to-one basis, or as a focus group. Interviews are easily adaptable to being run in person on a face-to-face basis, over the phone or via a 'virtual face-to-face' meeting over the Internet. Interviews are usually used on a small sample population to gather in-depth information about the subject under scrutiny. Data is often recorded on a digital voice recorder, by taking notes during the interview, video and occasionally even having an extra person present to take notes.

OBSERVATIONS

Observations can be a qualitative or quantitative data collection method depending on whether their purpose is part of a natural experiment, field experiment or laboratory/controlled experiment. Usually you would simply observe and record the variables relevant to your experiment in the appropriate setting carrying out any experiment-specific interactions if required. Part of making observations is collecting and recording measurements during laboratory/controlled experiments, which must be collected with the utmost care and attention. If you are using any technical equipment you must ensure it is in good working order, accurate, correctly calibrated and that you know how to use it.

SECONDARY DATA

Published literature, documents and records are usually referred to as secondary data collection as someone else has collected the information. This can be a relatively cheap source of data collection, which will usually help to inform you about your area of research.

QUESTIONNAIRES /SURVEYS

Questionnaires/surveys have become one of the cheapest methods of data collection to involve a large population.

Questionnaires/surveys are a method of gaining information about the characteristics of a population rather than in-depth information from an individual. Questionnaires/surveys can be conducted in person, over the phone, via post, email or through a link on the Internet.

NO
SHORT CUTS

There are no short cuts in collecting and recording data in an experiment.

You must plan ahead and pay attention to all the details. If something doesn't work out as you anticipated, it doesn't mean it's wrong. It's still a valid outcome if you have adhered to proper methods of conduct, data collection and recording.

Data collection can be something as simple as how many times you do something in a set period of time. This is called the frequency. This could be the number of times you look at your phone or watch or something of your choosing, in a set amount of time. Think about the best way of collecting and recording this data on the chart below. Once you have done this, consider what you might do with that data.

	Number of times activity performed each hour											
Activity	Hour 1	Hour 2	Hour 3	Hour 4	Hour 5	Hour 6	Hour 7	Hour 8	Hour 9	Hour 10	Hour 11	Hour 12

What could you do with this data?

....

....

....

....

....

....

....

....

....

....

To ensure you know everything you need to know about getting your data from experiments, please work through the following checklist.

☐ Do you understand what an experiment is? If not go back to page 9

☐ Do you understand why you need an experiment for your research? If not go back to page 21

☐ Do you know the differences between the main types of experiment and which one you need for your research? If not go back to page 37

☐ Do you know how to ensure your experiment is ethically appropriate? If not go back to page 51

HOW TO KNOW
YOU
ARE
DONE

CHECKPOINT

☐ Have you been able to consider if your experiment is reproducible?
If not go back to page 67

☐ Have you considered areas where you could minimise error in your
experiment? If not go back to page 79

☐ Are you able to recognise the different types of data you need to
collect for your experiment? If not go back to page 95

☐ Have you created a plan of how to collect data for your
experiment? If not go back to page 109

Glossary

Association   A relationship between things. More specifically, in research, this will refer to a relationship between objects or variables.

Bias   There are many forms of bias you should be aware of. This can simply mean a promotion or demotion of something or someone which can influence or impact your research results. This usually happens due to poor data collection techniques, incorrect or inadequate sampling, design or analysis.

Data collection   This is the process of collecting or gathering the data required for your research.

Ethics   This refers to the set of principles governing your conduct about what is right and wrong or acceptable or unacceptable in your research. Your institution will likely have an ethics committee who will be able to guide you on specific requirements.

Hypothesis, Alternate/Experimental A statement that predicts a relationship between an independent variable (causal) and dependent variable (outcome).

Hypothesis, Null A statement that predicts there is no relationship between an independent variable and dependent variable.

Qualitative This is a method of research, primarily exploratory, conducted in naturalistic settings which generates non-numerical data largely from observations, focus groups and interviews in order to gain an understanding of underlying reasons, opinions and motivations.

Quantitative This is a method of research, primarily used to formulate facts. It generates numerical data or data that can be recoded into a format for statistical analysis, largely from surveys, structured interviews, longitudinal studies and systematic observations. It enables the researcher to explore relationships between and among variables using numeric data.

Reliability This is the consistency and dependability of a measure, procedure or instrument in gathering data. It is also the extent to which a measurement, result or calculation can be believed to be accurate and correct.

Validity This refers to the extent to which data and findings are sound and accurate reflections of reality. It refers to both design and methods of research.

Validity, Ecological This refers to how far you can generalise the findings of your research into real-life settings.

Variable, Confounding A variable that has not been accounted for within your study, but has an effect on your results.

Variable, Dependent This is the output or outcome variable. It is the response, the thing you measure the changes of to check if the treatment or intervention had an effect. The values of the dependent variable are dependent on the manipulation of the independent variable.

Variable, Extraneous Any variable you are not studying in your experiment that interferes with the relationship between the independent and dependent variable and must be controlled.

Variable, Independent The conditions of an experiment that are manipulated by the researcher. The thing you change to assess if there are any changes in your dependent variable.